Edited by

Crystal Cheatham
Will Remigio
Adam Evers

Illustrated & designed by

Will Remigio

In collaboration with
Our Bible App & believr

believr.

Bemba
Press
AN IMPRINT OF
OUR BIBLE INC. 2021

Bemba Press
Philadelphia

QUEER HANDS
OF GOD

Edited by Crystal Cheatham, Will Remigio, Adam Evers.
Illustrated by Will Remigio

Bemba Press
An imprint of Our Bible, Inc.
Philadelphia

First edition Published November 2021

Printed in the United States of America

For information about special discounts for bulk purchases, please contact
Bemba Press at hi@ourbibleapp.com or visit our website at www.ourbibleapp.com

ISBN 978-1-7370884-6-2 (Black & White & Hard Cover)
ISBN 978-1-7370884-7-9 (Hard Cover & Full Color)
ISBN 978-1-7370884-8-6 (eBook)

STORIES

"Where the mind goes energy flows"
- Ernest Holmes

God works through human hands.

Walk through any church and the stained glass windows tell stories of the Holy Spirit being served to humanity by mortal hands. These stories remind us that people are conduits for the good and the holy things that make their way into this world. Yet if you are LGBTQ+ like we are (Crystal, Will & Adam), you know there can be a disparity. How often are the helpers and saints depicted in that radiant glass LGBTQ+ people? If they are not written about, drawn, or remembered, did they ever truly exist?

In this too, representation matters.

As creators and friends, we've come together with the voices of 30 storytellers to stain some glass of our own, or maybe even shatter the glass that keeps queer depictions of God out of sacred spaces.

As inspired by the imaginings of Will Remigio, Queer Hands of God attempts—in a very small way—to illustrate the invisible ways the Holy Spirit moves among queer folk. These Queer Hands of God are life savers, the support beams of chosen family, the gentle reminders to have hope when we're down and out, financiers when the bill is due, doorstops when the door is closing and finally—as we like to call them—angels when a miracle is all that will save us.

As you read this book, may these stories renew your spiritual energies. Take heart in knowing that we, as queer individuals, are not beyond God's affection. May you find restorative oneness with the Creator, seeing your hands as flowing extensions of God's love in a loveless world.

Go with God,

Crystal, Will & Adam

Storytellers

The storytellers in this book are people, whether queer or straight, who shared their experience encountering an LGBTQ+ person.

Queer Hands of God

The Queer Hands of God in this book are people who identify as LGBTQ+, who played a significant role in the life of the storyteller.

People info

People's, pronouns, illustrations, and Instagram usernames (Ex: @believrapp) are displayed in the book with permission from all parties. Magical unicorn animals and pseudo names are in the place of those who wished to remain anonymous.

Accessibility

The eBook of Queer Hands of God supports enhanced accessibility features that work with screen readers and other assistive technologies.

We want to honor and thank our incredible community. Each of us made unique contributions to enable this project and–oh–how precious your gifts are.

Believr Tuesday Night Meetup - **Storytelling**
Believr Thursday Night Bible Study - **Storytelling**
David Castillon-Mendoza (any/todos) - **Outreach**
David H. Collins (he/him) - **Creative Support**
Evan Doyle (he/him) - **Editing + PR**
Keegan Osinski (she/her) - **Editing**
Omar Rivera-Valentin (he/him) - **Editing**
Queer Hands of God - **Storytelling**
Storytellers - **Storytelling**

DEDICATION

For the troubled beloved who was misinformed and told that
being queer is a result of trauma. For the one who sadly
believes that our queerness disconnects us from God. May
this book honor the lives of our LGBTQ+ community as we
collectively embrace a call to live out loud & live out love.

Hannah experiences the simple graces of friendship and a garden.

Hannah

Storyteller

(she/her)
@hannahabonner

Susan

Queer Hand of God

(she/her)

Mary

Queer Hand of God

(she/her)

After years of fight and struggle, Hannah is welcomed into rest and nurtured by the loving kindness of Mary and Susan and their garden.

I long for the dirt when my soul grows weary. For the soil. For the earth. It's the garden where I find myself, take my broken places, and—along with God—put myself back together. There is an excitement for me in the thought that life itself began in a garden, and our lives can always begin anew there as well. My faith is rooted in a belief in life overcoming death and a God mistaken for a gardener. With every seed that I bury, I am reminded of the ripping apart that happens as a seed becomes something else—perhaps a flower to bring delight, a tomato to bring sustenance, an herb to flavor life.

When I left Texas, after years of confronting racist violence in a way that brought threats to my own life, the last thing I thought I would find was a garden. It is not that I did not long for one, but I did not expect one. I was going to the desert, not far from the border, simply trying to imagine a life beyond survival. I decided that after all the times I lived when no one else thought I would, that now I would truly *live*. It felt as if I had given my life; yet, rather than losing it, I had somehow received it back. I was determined to cherish that gift.

When I arrived in Arizona, I found an image of cherishing and nurturing that went beyond what I had witnessed before. I was befriended by two women, Mary and Susan, who were clergywomen like myself and very much in love with one another. They welcomed me into their backyard and shared their garden with me. I observed its rows and vines and paths and the contours of their interactions with one another as well.

They offered me brunch, and as each one spoke, the other would look at her with such admiration and reverence and desire to protect. After a decade together, they still could not keep their eyes off each other. In their tender glances, they cherished every word the other spoke with such gentleness and reverence.

I needed this. I needed to witness this simplicity. I needed to know that we can be more than fighters, that life can be more than survival. As a queer woman born into a church, home, and school that condemned every part of who I was, I had been fighting not to be crushed every moment of my life.

As queer clergywomen, our very existence is resistance. We are a living, breathing act of defiance to the rules that say we are not supposed to exist. Yet, here we are. With every breath we inhale, with every beat of our hearts, with every step that we take, we never cease to be resistance embodied. We never get a day off from who we are.

After a lifetime of this fight to dismantle patriarchy and racism, I needed this body that I live in to be more than a battle. I needed this life that had been spared to be more than a sacrifice. I needed to know that we could be more than fighters.

I needed to know that we are gardeners too. We are those who plant, those who grow, those who tend, those who nurture, those who protect. I needed to know that though the earth may be hard and dry— especially here in the desert—there will indeed be a harvest.

When I did not lose my life, I decided that I would live it. But I needed Susan to show me where she grows her green beans. I needed Mary to show me the netting she uses to protect what Susan planted. I needed to witness their giddy delight in being around each other.

In their love, Mary and Susan showed me a vision beyond the fight. They showed me what we are fighting for in the end.

As queer people, we are beauty, grace, persistence, and love. We are tenderness, patience, gentleness, and kindness. I know this because I have seen it now, and that can never be taken away from me.

"As queer people, we are beauty, grace, persistence, and love. We are tenderness, patience, gentleness, and kindness. I know this because I have seen it now, and that can never be taken away from me."

-Hannah

Ophelia sees possibilities for her future reflected in Serena's beautiful family.

Ophelia

Storyteller

(she/her)
@opxihk

Serena

Queer Hand of God

(she/her)
@lovespellie

Thanks to the path Serena forged for herself through struggle, Ophelia feels able to create a queer Asian-American life of her own.

It had taken fifteen years to get here: my mother is seated at my dining table, her face lit up by the glow of my phone. She can't hide her smile. She whispers because my wife is sleeping and my father is getting ready for bed. "I've never seen an Asian lesbian family before. So this is what your family will look like."

"Sort of," I say, and the treasure of this moment is not lost on me. She's looking at photos of my friend Serena Cerezo-Poon and her family–her wife and children. Maybe she sees in their children her own children–my brother and me–and the children her children will one day have.

The glow of my mother's smile. The recognition in her softened face. I owe these and more to Serena.

Serena didn't set out to blaze a trail by living authentically. But I and countless other LGBTQ Asian Americans have walked paths where Serena has gone and where she still walks with us.

Serena is a wife and mother, a Chinese American, and an auntie to a vast network fo LGBTQ Asian Americans seeking affirmation and self-sufficiency – often taking to online community to find one another and seek alternatives to in-person, white-dominated LGBTQ spaces and unaffirming Christian ethnic community. Serena is a daughter to parents who have not received her queerness with the acceptance that Serena has helped my own parents to reach.

She likens her parents to the Chinese Christian versions of Hillary and Bill Clinton: well-known, revered, and influential in the vast world of conservative Chinese missions. Themselves missionaries and pastors, they rejected Serena's queer identity. Decades after she came out, Serena's parents are still unaffirming.

Perhaps it's our trouble as people who believe in a three-day resurrection that we long for every relationship to be made right and every heartbreak to heal. Not every chapter of every story ends neatly, tied up with a bow of resolution.

But in our pain is an alchemical choice: we can choose to transmit or transform our hurt. And Serena lives a life of transformation. Although she had few queer Asian American role models in her own growing-up journey, she is comfortable with her own visibility and works to ensure the visibility of her kin so that today's young queer Asian Americans have role models. She co-leads workshops on queer Asian family dynamics, has generously told her story to the benefit of those who might see her, and facilitates online queer Asian Christian communities with tenderness and deftness.

And whereas she has experienced broken covenants from her family of origin, she has chosen a path of love for her own family–co-raising with her wife two children who are gentle, kind, and affirmed of their parents' wide-open love. At the same time, she leaves the door open for the possibility, without expectation, of a healing relationship with her own parents. It's this fierce devotion to love and non-attachment to expectation that have provided a blueprint for my own healing relationship with my family of origin. And it's Serena's own family that has shown my mother that my own is someday possible, God willing.

Serena lives out countless queer spiritual gifts, and she especially embodies the queer spiritual gift of alchemy. This is a magic that God has gifted us queer beloveds: the power to transform experiences of exclusion and pain into kinship and kin-dom.

Derrick's friendship with Scott changed the way he thought, worked, and

Derrick

Storyteller

(he/him)
@dlweston

Melinda

Queer Hand of God

(he/him)

Becoming close friends with a queer Christian gave Derrick an entirely different perspective on the way he did ministry and related to others as an ally.

Seminary was a formative time for me, though not in the ways that I expected. I chose my seminary, San Francisco Theological Seminary, despite the warnings that it was "liberal." I honestly didn't know what that meant, but I was eager to find out. I was quickly introduced to a world of historical critical theory, gender neutral names for the Divine, and the subtle hint that maybe I didn't have to vote Republican. I was also introduced to many LGBTQ Christians determined to figure out what their place was in the church. Just months before I left for seminary, a friend came out to me, and I uttered the horrid cliché that God "loved the sinner but hated the sin". I don't know that I'll ever live that down.

By the end of my first semester, I was in a completely different place. Another close friend came out to me that Christmas break and by that time I had met so many amazing gay and lesbian friends who were wrestling with systems that didn't know what to do with them, that all I could do was embrace him and tell him that he was deeply loved. For the next few months, I tried to walk side by side with him as he faced the backlash of coming out to friends and family including a conservative pastor father who said some truly awful things to him. Even as I was figuring out all my views, I knew that what I was seeing in response to my friend wasn't love. Still, I was waffling, knowing that I needed to move beyond tolerance.

My second year of seminary, Scott and his husband Jeff joined the community. Scott was incredibly likeable; funny, charming, and I loved that we could shift between talking about college football to talking about Gilmore Girls. In my third year, Scott and Jeff moved into the apartment above my now ex and me, and for a semester, Scott rode shotgun as I drove the seminary van from our Marin County campus to Berkeley. It was during one of those drives that a major shift happened in me. I was having problems in my ordination process, but in hindsight, most of those problems were self-made by my arrogance and stubbornness. Scott was having issues in his ordination process because, at that time, our denomination wasn't yet ordaining LGBTQ pastors officially.

Scott continued to go through the process with grace and good humor, both, I think because of the strength of his sense of call and because of his deep and evident love for the church. While I was bitching about imagined slights I was enduring at the hands of the system, Scott was faithfully trying to work in and with a system that was essentially saying, "we don't want you."

That year Scott was a chaplain's assistant and, in that role, arranged for the Shower of Stoles exhibit to be brought to the school. The exhibit is a collection of clerical stoles and other sacred items recognizing the lives of LGBTQ faith leaders from nearly thirty denominations spread over three continents. Along with the exhibit, Scott invited the Rev. Dr. Jane Spahr to come and preach for a chapel service. (Scott would later serve as Rev. Spahr's defense when charges were brought against her for performing the marriage of two women.) During that service, which Scott facilitated, I had one of my many conversion experiences. In that space, I dedicated myself to being the best ally I could possibly be.

I don't have much to be proud of from my brief stint in pastoral ministry. I did, however, lead the last church I served through the process of officially becoming an openly LGBTQ affirming congregation.

I emphasized to the congregation the importance of not just letting our support be implied, but that it was time to be vocally and visually in support of those who have so often been hurt by the church.

I don't know if Scott knew how much his friendship had an impact on me. I don't know if he realized that watching him navigate his struggles put mine into perspective. I don't know if he realized that his quiet influence would change my life. But I am grateful for him, and even as I am away from church leadership, I strive to let my LGBTQ family know that they are loved, by me and by God.

"While I was bitching about imagined slights I was enduring at the hands of the system, Scott was faithfully trying to work in and with a system that was essentially saying, "we don't want you."

-Derrick

Through confusing times, Adam showed him a clear path for understanding himself.

Luke

Storyteller

(he/him)
@las_thebos

Adam

Queer Hand of God

(he/him)

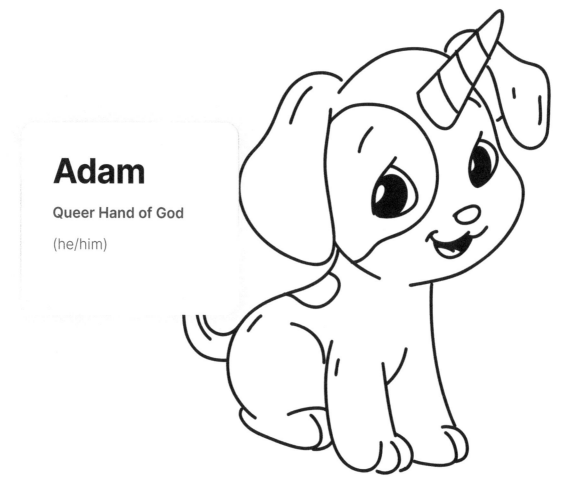

Luke thought he was alone in the closet, but upon his decision to come out, a new friend welcomed him into community and reinforced his faith in God.

In 2017, I was living in a dorm during my sophomore year at a Christian university. Life felt like an emotional roller coaster. I was clueless about what to believe in terms of my faith, and I didn't know how much longer I could keep secret about being gay. On the 3rd of September (I remember the exact day), I couldn't carry the weight any longer. I heard God impressing on my heart that I needed to confide in my resident director. Her response astonished me. She asked me, 'How can I love you best?' Two weeks later, she introduced me to Adam, someone who was open about his bisexuality while still maintaining his faith in Jesus. He made time to connect with me, and eventually introduced me to a supportive community of people with whom I could let my guard down and speak openly about my life, free of shame. Self-acceptance began to shine during a time which felt like a crisis.

In her despair, Nicole walked with her towards a peaceful journey with God.

Tiara

Storyteller

(she/her)
@iamtlynn2

Nicole

Queer Hand of God

(she/her)
@nicoleblacksonspeaks

Tiara was unemployed, heartbroken, and unhoused. Nicole invited her to a LGBTQ+ affirming community where Tiara found a home and began to love herself.

In 2016, I was transitioning between jobs, healing from an abusive relationship that ended abruptly, and couch hopping while unhoused. All of this happened after my parents shunned me for coming out as a bisexual woman. Amidst all this despair and shame, God used my friend Nicole to provide me peace and solace. She invited me to her church, an affirming church, and for the first time ever, I felt that God showed me what the Church was always meant to be and feel like. I saw people from every walk of life: LGBQ+, trans, unhoused, Black, white, and so many others. Their warmth and sincerity quenched my soul's need for acceptance and compassion. As I bore witness to their unapologetic worship of God, my heart had found a home. During this time, Nicole showed me how to love myself and guided me in my search for meaning and authenticity.

After his heartbreak, Omar felt unworthy and unstable. Then, he met Will & Tiara on his journey toward healing, self-love, and self-worth.

Omar

Storyteller

(he/him)
@mr.o_valentin

Will

Queer Hand of God

(any)
@bluemarble___

Tiara

Queer Hand of God

(she/her)
@iamtlynn2

Omar was in an abusive relationship that made him feel as if he was unforgivable and unredeemable in God's eyes. Thankfully, God placed Will & Tiara in Omar's life. Their love helped Omar reconnect with God.

In mid-2019, I had just gotten out of an abusive relationship. My former partner was constantly telling me that I was too sensitive, needed a thicker skin, was not man enough, and was not worthy enough. I believed everything I was being told and his words continued to haunt me even past the end of the relationship. Then, God placed two wonderful friends in my life that showed me how great God's love is for me. Will introduced me to a bi-weekly LGBTQ+ Bible study group called FUEL, which is where I met Tiara. They quickly became my family while I lived in Philadelphia. With their support, love, and encouragement, I was reminded that God had a deeper purpose for my life, that I was worthy of being loved, and that I was enough. I don't know where I would be had God not brought Will and Tiara into my life, and I am thankful every day that their presence in my life brought me closer to God again.

During a faith crisis, Joseph's reality was shaken. When he met Austin, a never-before-seen side of Jesus was revealed.

Joseph

Storyteller

(he/him/they/them)
@c.josephlee_

Austin

Queer Hand of God

(he/him)
@as_gaskins

Joseph lived in a hostile Christian setting and struggled to reconcile his ideals of a loving God with what he observed in his church during the Black Lives Matter protests. Then, Austin showed them a God that sides with the oppressed.

Being gay and living in a Southern Baptist community, it was difficult for me to feel comfortable in God's love. Doing ministry had always appealed to me, but I felt inadequate. Thinking that a heterosexual marriage would solve all my problems, my plan was to marry a woman and help other queer people follow a similar path. Despite all the internalized homophobia, my gut told me there was something off about how my church viewed God. They talked negatively against Black Lives Matter protests and upheld insensitive political values, which left me questioning God's integrity and love. Then, as a result of prayer, Austin came into my life. He helped me understand that the confusion I felt was a form of heartbreak. I was having a sad realization about the current loveless state of the Christian church. Moreover, Austin was an openly queer man who lived out a divine calling for ministry. He embodied everything I never thought was possible. Through his steady and patient guidance, I arrived at a place where my faith and my life slowly began to feel whole again. I didn't leave the church in totality, and I hope to be able to return to some kind of ministry in an affirming congregation eventually, but for now I have stopped attending church in person on a regular basis. I got connected with a church in Florida where I went to school and still occasionally watch their services on their livestream, but in general I'm not in a place right now where I can swallow my anxiety in church settings. I have embraced my own queerness, and I'm in the process of coming out. I've been slowly revealing my queerness to the world, but I have fully embraced it for myself.

"He helped me understand that the confusion I felt was a form of heartbreak. I was having a sad realization about the current loveless state of the Christian church."

-Joseph

Despite their different backgrounds, Rebecca and Lane forge a friendship that changes Rebecca's outlook.

Rebecca P.

Storyteller

(she/her)
@tealvixenette

Lane

Queer Hand of God

(they/them)

Getting to know Lane helped Rebecca question the things she had been taught and open her eyes to more diverse ways of living.

Our partners have travelled half the world together. Their pasts are part of a deep-rooted community. We were the newcomers, the ones finding our way in. Once a year, this group of liberal faith dwellers, explorers of The Way and seekers of community under the Holy Spirit would gather at a Faith, Arts and Activism festival in central England. My love had hardly missed one in twenty years. However, I'd never slept in a tent.

Neither had Lane. Yet we were both keen to try for our partners, and for our own spiritual development. We were enlivened by the joy we saw in their eyes as they spoke, and in the promise of a deeper communion with them. So I bought a sleeping bag, Lane borrowed a camping mat, and we said yes to our first experience of many that followed.

The first evening was blissful. Sitting with a drink in my hand, on the edge of a soft glade under gentle lamps and fluttering bunting, my soul was at peace. I looked over at Lane, across the circle of tents with children playing in the centre, and they tentatively smiled back at me. As we settled in for the evening and said our goodnights, there was some nervousness in the air – not least because my love's tent was barely bigger than a postage stamp and he'd bought an air bed to treat me! Oh, how we would laugh as we tried to squeeze in there.

Of course, the air bed was a nod to my total inability to rough it. In fact, I had a total inability to face anything outside of my standard frame of reference: that of a "good Christian girl," marriage between one man and one woman, sex only within that framework, only drink a little and never do drugs, definitely don't go camping at a festival with a group of LGBTQ+ progressives who may partake in all sorts of suspicious herbals, will definitely get up to yoga, and are sharing tents "in sin!" This was not me. But something was stirring in me that perhaps wanted it to be me. Thought it could be me. Thought perhaps all that wasn't as wrong as I'd been led to believe it was. And the person I was identifying the most with, feeling the most drawn to this weekend, was the person I had been taught by the faith of my family to keep away from, because they were choosing to live in sin.

We sat and talked a lot the next day, over jazz, jokes and judicious discussions of protests. As the day wore on, we began sharing about our lives. Lane talked about their conservative Christian family, the journey to acceptance of their queerness which was still in very early stages, and the challenges around their parents' acceptance of their wonderful same-sex partner. I talked about my equally conservative Christian family, my recent divorce and the journey back from the depression which had almost cost me my life - because staying in a toxic relationship was preferable to the unforgivable sin of divorce, in my muddled up, evangelically influenced, theologically unsound and infantile interpretation of God's guidance for my life. We talked about Church, Lane's struggle to engage, my struggle to stay within.

I realised I had made my first true friendship and connection with a queer person. And it was beautiful. Lane was just like me. Vulnerable, shaped by their childhood; hopeful, loving a future into being. Lane deserved everything I deserved. Acceptance, equity, to walk down the street holding her love's hand and it being the most normal thing in the world. Across that field of faith I saw many LGBTQ+ couples openly expressing their love, and it was good. God saw it, and it was good.

God saw Lane and I, opening our hearts to each other, and blessed us. What has grown from that, the love and friendship, support, acceptance and allyship, is good.

Lane taught me not just to accept, but to embrace. Not just to have intention, but to mean it. Not just to say the words, but walk the walk. I am an activist and an ally because of Lane.

"Lane taught me not just to accept, but to embrace. Not just to have intention, but to mean it. Not just to say the words, but walk the walk."

-Rebecca

Learning to open up to her wife was an exercise in learning to open up to God.

Gennifer

Storyteller

(she/her)

Alley

Queer Hand of God

(she/her)

Gennifer recounts meeting Alethea and how love can overcome fear.

When we first exchanged numbers under a streetlamp, she told me her full name was Alethea. "That means *truth*," my dilettante study of biblical Greek enabled me to blurt out.

Apparently this blew her mind so much that she walked away thinking, "I think I just met my future wife." At least that's how she tells the story over and over again.

For me, it wasn't quite like that. Two months later, I came around – sort of. We were drinking Hennessy in a mutual friend's kitchen and she told the story of how she became Catholic. The teachers didn't want her in church, so they outed her to the priest. He pulled her aside and said he'd heard she might be living an "alternative lifestyle."

"You know what, Father," she told the priest, "we had a Bible reading this past week about the lady who committed adultery and the disciples were going to stone her, and Jesus said, 'He who throws the first stone has no sin.' It's so easy to attack somebody else for something because you don't want to look at yourself." The priest replied, "I'm sorry that you've been experiencing this at my church. Can I give you a hug?" And she said, "Yes," and he gave her a hug.

The rest of that night is a blur, as I moved from Hennessy to whiskey. At some point she helped me stumble up the stairs and we slept in separate rooms of the house. When I woke up, I was in love with her.

But I've always had a bit of trouble trusting what I love. God, for instance. There are moments when I'm listening to Alley pray from her Pieta book and a deep peace opens in me like a blooming rose in my heart. I believe the words I heard in Sunday school long ago: *Don't be afraid, I am with you.* I believe I could walk into that darkest valley, the future, and fear no evil.

And even when those moments pass, I have one belief that's never shaken: God put her in my life. I quip that she's my ride or die, because if she weren't my ride, I would die. My demons would catch me by the heel. They're more or less under control now. The binge drinking problem I developed as a still-closeted college student has been dialed down to the occasional extra glass of wine. But I don't take my newfound strength for granted.

So why have I been frightened to stand before my God and swear I'll go where she goes?

I was always so used to going it alone. I zeroed in on the flaws of others, bracing to protect myself. I forgot to think about my weaknesses, mistaking God's mercy for my own cunning.

Alley's only real flaw is that she loves others so much that she doesn't leave enough love for herself. I've pleaded with her to think of her mental and physical health while caretaking for multiple members of her family. I've made some headway over the years, but she is who she is. If you're one of her people, that's it – she'll follow you straight into hell.

I'm drawn to the idea of marriage because I think every person deserves someone who will stay at their side no matter what. We've got God for that, but sometimes flesh and blood needs flesh and blood. And I met a woman who walks in the footsteps of Christ.

Alethea, my future wife: no one has ever been more worthy of a name.

Father Rodger's witness gives Kevin the confidence he needs as a queer minister.

Kevin

Storyteller

(he/him)
@ktracey95

Father Rodger

Queer Hand of God

(he/him)

As a new minister, Kevin is uncertain of his gifts and call, but Father Rodger, with his wisdom and experience, encourages Kevin in his work.

Father Rodger and I sat across from each other, my sermon manuscript splayed across the table in front of me. As a first-year seminarian at the church he was called to as rector, I preached once a month. And as a first-year seminarian, every time I stepped into the pulpit, I felt an overwhelming sense of dread. The sparsely attended early-morning service that had ended just a few minutes ago had not been an exception to that dread.

After a few notes and corrections for the second service, Rodger stood, his smile warm as his eyes. He reached the door and paused, turning to face me again.

"You've been given the authority to preach the Gospel. Embrace that call and preach," he offered, a firm kindness lining his voice.

Father Rodger was an openly gay priest serving in Philadelphia. He was ordained thirty or so years ago and had been quietly present alongside the battle across the Episcopal Church for the inclusion of LGBTQ+ priests. His ministry in Philadelphia had been one of inclusion and welcome. During the height of the HIV/AIDS crisis, he was one of the few priests in the area that would care for and ultimately bury the people who died from the disease.

Father Rodger's story was one he kept close to himself, guarded and private. Yet, his care and love poured from him, into everyone and everything around him.

When I walked up the steps to his parish the first time, I was a newly-out first-year seminarian, unsure of myself, my church, and so much more. I knew God was calling me to ministry, and I knew that call included my full self, but I didn't know how.

Rodger showed me.

His words of encouragement on that day in his office have been a refrain I hold in my heart – one I repeat over and over again.

Father Roger allowed me to use my voice – to preach the truths I had come to know – and to share the Good News as I had experienced it. His guidance allowed me to find my voice: a voice that did not shy away from who I am, but rather embraced it. He spoke of messiness, heartbreak, and pain from the pulpit. And he spoke of love, grace, and beauty.

His own experiences of exclusion and isolation showed him how to preach love into a world that longed for hate.

Something shifted in me that day in Roger's office. I let some of my own walls down and I continue to do so today. It's a slow process – unlearning and relearning things always is.

God showed up in that moment. God moved in that room, and the Holy Spirit offered a breath. Breath that comforted me. Breath that guided me. Breath that affirmed my authority.

Father Roger's words that morning continue to ground me. They continue to be a part of the prayer I offer each time I step into the pulpit. They continue to remind me of the history that stands behind me as a queer person. They continue to remind me of the future that stands brightly before us.

And they continue to be a reminder that the Good News of the Gospel is for anyone and everyone.

Gaines felt like the school outcast until Micah joined him. Refusing conversion therapy, together they sought another path.

Gaines

Storyteller

(he/him)
@gainestaylor86

Micah

Queer Hand of God

(He/him)

Attending a hostile Christian university, Gaines resisted traditional beliefs about his sexual identity. Micah came into his life to remind him to wrestle with the unanswered questions.

In 2005, during my freshman year at Liberty University, I found myself in a setting where I did not feel safe to ask any questions. Studying in a non-affirming environment, I felt turned off by the leadership. In fact, it felt like their counsel brought more hopelessness than hope. This couldn't be what God wished for me. "How could this be the only way?" I thought. I can't remember how Micah came into my life, but somehow we became a safe place for each other as we navigated the self-discovery of being gay Christians at that school. Micah and I became closer friends and prayed for each other while still figuring out what redemption looked like for a couple of outcasts like ourselves. Knowing him helped to ease the feelings of alienation in a school with thousands of students. Simply having another person to walk the journey felt reassuring. Today, I look back at that experience and see that Christ showed up then. God didn't want me to walk this path alone and provided me with a friend for the ride. That's just how God works sometimes. When we least expect it, others may enter our lives to remind us that we are fully loved as fully queer.

Chelle offers you her experience as an invitation to unify all of God's children.

Chelle

Storyteller

(she/they)
@treatmetoafeast_holybadass

You

Hand of God

(any)

I don't have one single angel I can label as my "hand of God," rather I can attest to being swept into this wonderful movement of redefining social boundaries in order to be more inclusive. Earlier this year, the Wall Street Journal reported that "to encourage better respect towards people's boundaries, event hosts are using colored accessories to help communicate their comfort around physical touch." Like traffic lights, green means go, yellow means caution and red is a hard stop. When my employer adopted the practice for conferences I proudly made my position clear—my lanyard choice was yellow. I really enjoyed the idea of consent before touch. As I understand, many who are LGBTQ+ rely on consensual touches to feel safe and welcome. I didn't realize how much I needed this as well.

That social growth spurt was one of many to come. I soon realized the importance of pronouns. On LinkedIn, I began articulating my pronouns as she/her. As a cisgendered woman, I now know that articulating that creates a safer environment for gender-queer and nonbinary people. It means that no one should assume they know how you identify.

The third thing I've learned from LGBTQ+ people is that I am not bound to the family I was born with. In fact, I have agency to go out and bond with people not of my blood and call them home. I know this term to be *found* or *chosen family*. Before my *found family* found me, I failed at loving everyone just as they were—as God created them to be. Fortunately, God waited at the edges of my comfort zone, knowing that I would come to embrace new connections online. With my defenses down, I virtually held hands with and traded laughter and tears across tables and sofas with people whose worlds I would never have intersected with otherwise. I let go of my defenses and let the light in. I allowed myself to find joy in the unknown, to not let difference scare me, and ultimately to nurture and be nurtured by people that I previously would have labeled "other" and been "othered" by.

As a woman of African descent often found in white American spaces, I am acutely aware of how left out feels. But in Matthew 11:28 Jesus says, "Come to me, all of you..." Is that not the heart of inclusion? If for any reason you are unclear, return to the Gospel and study Jesus' words.

People of faith, if we are to be what we profess, it's time to submit to God's will, and heal the relationships we have (or don't) with the queer community. They see us shaming God and ourselves every time our backs turn and our eyes close. However, like Bartimeus in Mark's Gospel it is possible for us to see and be seen.

It's time for conviction. We are overdue in embracing and welcoming ALL God's children or must confess that we are not yet whom we claim to be. This is a prayer of gratitude for so many who patiently held my hands and my heart as I edged beyond my tiny corner of the Universe. Faith and mothering birthed within me an ever-broadening definition of ALL, with neither qualifiers nor special circumstances under which we might make exception. I continue to grow. May it ever be so.

That is the Gospel as it is. If you are not there today, honor the path of grace, and you will, with God's help, begin seeing yourself as one among all of God's beloved.

This is my love letter to All of God's Children.

Redeeming God, hear our prayers.

Ellie felt she couldn't be Christian and gay. Matt invited her to embrace a bold new faith that integrates every part of herself.

Ellie

Storyteller

(she/her)
@ellieoconnor13

Matt

Queer Hand of God

(he/him)
@yogamatt13

She felt accepted at school, but coming back home for break forced her to resolve her feelings for women. Matt offered her strength from his experience.

I grew up in Southwest Michigan. For my entire life, I felt tension between my sexual identity and my faith. Matt was an openly gay guy I had known since high school. We had done Young Life ministry back in the day, encouraging so many young people to feel loved; but here I was, not feeling this love in my own life. Matt helped a lot by offering me tons of helpful books and bringing me to the Queer Christian Fellowship Conference. He taught me to question fixed traditions and invited me to seek who God was for me. Of course I was afraid of the critics, but Matt was so confident in who he was and had no doubts about God's stamp of approval over his life. I used to think my salvation and heavenly calling was to become straight and no longer struggle with being gay. Today, my faith is vibrant and full of wonder, and I'm gay. Sure, my faith is a little different than others'; but it is my own and I'm secure in it. I will forever be grateful for the freedom Matt gave me.

The visibility and representation of a lesbian pastor gives Candace permission to be herself.

Candice

Storyteller

(she/her)
@Godly_andgay

Pastor Pam

Queer Hand of God

(she/her)

Candace wasn't expecting much when she first heard Pam preach, but her knowledge and character inspired Candace to love like Jesus.

I was living in San Diego, California and serving in the Marine Corps. It was 2004, during the height of Don't Ask, Don't Tell. Like most closeted Marines I longed for an outlet, a place where I could just be me, without the fear of being outed. I found that refuge in the most unlikely of places for me: a church. Prior to enlisting, I had no interest in religion. I hadn't stepped foot in a church since my grandmother's funeral several years prior. However, this was an affirming church that welcomed people like me, and when given the chance, I quickly joined and became involved in the music ministry.

I had been a member for a few months when our pastor invited one of her friends from Kentucky to preach. I honestly didn't expect much. But this preacher challenged every bias I had regarding good preaching. Born and raised in a black Baptist church, I believed that good preaching only came from older black men who carried towels to wipe the sweat from their brows. Pam Ogilvie was none of those things, so I was convinced and prepared for her to bore me to tears.

As part of the praise team, I took my place at the front of the church where I had a clear view of everyone in the sanctuary. I will admit I was intrigued when I caught a glimpse of the pastor's friend dancing, jumping, and shouting during praise and worship. My intrigue turned to inspiration when it was time for the sermon. I remember how Pastor Pam walked to the wooden podium. She was full of confidence, yet visibly humble. She prayed an earnest prayer and began to deliver a sermon that blew my mind, and solidified in my heart that one day I would learn to do what she did. I'd never heard anyone preach the way she did that day. She taught me more in thirty minutes than I had learned in all of my years in church. I was amazed.

What was even more amazing to me was that she was a lesbian. This woman who undeniably was anointed to preach, who operated in the gifts of the Holy Spirit, loved like I loved. People say that representation matters, and I know just how true that is. In fact, representation doesn't just matter, representation gives permission. Representation empowers. Representation opens minds and hearts.

To me, Pastor Pam Ogilvie exemplified what a gay Christian pastor looked like. In addition to her preaching style, she displayed the love of God in a way that shocked me. It was customary for the church to have food whenever a guest pastor would visit. The guest, along with the leadership of the church would sit at a "head table" or place of honor. Pastor Pam forfeited her seat of honor to sit with the congregation. From what little I knew about Jesus at the time, I knew that she was living the faith that she proclaimed. I also knew that if I were to be a pastor some day, I too would display the same level of humility and love.

I became a student, and Pastor Pam the instructor. I went to seminary to learn what she knew. When she would preach I would hang on every word, and I still do. All these years later, even after starting my own church, I still call Pastor Pam for wisdom and guidance. I still sit at her feet. I am honored that she now views me as a trusted friend and colleague. I owe so much to her. She broke down the barriers of my biases, which in turn freed me to follow my call to the fullest. Her authenticity and visibility in turn gave me permission to live authentically too. My prayer is that I represent God as well as Pastor Pam Ogilvie.

Whitley felt dispirited about leading worship as a gay woman. When she met David, her heart sang a new song of gratitude.

Whitley

Storyteller

(she/her)
@whit.ly

David

Queer Hand of God

(any/todos)
@dguadalupex

Whitley led worship at her church, but never felt fully loved by God until she came out of the closet. Meeting David gave her a newfound appreciation for her gift for music and life.

I was at my wits' end, feeling tired of fighting. For years, I had been at war with myself, thinking I had to choose to between being gay or feeling loved by God. Then one day, I met David at a meetup hosted by believr. He sent me a message joking about how my video background looked like a Hillsong worship session. After I told him I led worship at my church, we chatted about doing a worship night at believr. I thought to myself, wow, I've never worshiped with a group of queer people before. I agreed to do it. Looking back at this experience, I realize it was here that I found the strength to come out of the closet. For the first time in a long time, I felt peace about being a lesbian. David helped me as I transitioned church congregations, and encouraged me to trust that God was genuinely interested in the real me.

In losing their marriage, Noel finds a new family and a new name.

Noel

Storyteller

(they/them)
@mxnoellyheartland

Jarrett

Queer Hand of God

(he/him)
@jarrettactor

Sam

Queer Hand of God

(he/him)
@iam_samlandis

Coming out and losing their marriage was traumatic for Noel, but Sam and Jarrett gave them a safe place to land and support in picking up the pieces and making something new.

"I think you need to leave. Noah is going to come and get you and bring you to my house. Can you meet him outside in a half hour?" It was an out of body experience as I typed, "Yes" back to Sam. I looked around at my home for the last time I would see it in that state. I wasn't sure if or when I would see my beloved pets again, so I got down to their level and squeezed them with tears streaming, assuring them I wasn't leaving because I didn't love them.

When the evening took a very unexpected turn, involving police involvement for my protection, I remember lying on the floor, feeling the fibers of the carpet, and crying. It felt like I was crying out months of uncertainty and fear in addition to heartbreak. I remember my friends getting on the floor with me, sitting around me, allowing me to cling to their bodies for as long as I needed, and assuring me they weren't going to leave. If I had to describe the experience in one word, it would be "family."

Queer friends and LGBTQIA+ chosen family had always been an integral part of my world, especially since coming out to my family had essentially eaten away at what was left of our relationship after a conservative fundamentalist cult upbringing. Losing a marriage is even harder without parents to scoop up the broken pieces and help you put yourself back together. I had been very private about some of the details happening behind closed doors off and on during my marriage, but two people I had opened up to were Sam and Jarrett. Sam and I always have had a close bond, especially regarding social justice issues. We share a passion for all kinds of activism education and projects. Jarrett is someone who always makes space to discuss mental health, and shares some of his own experiences, which helped me when I struggled with decisions I never expected to face.

In the Christian Bible, there are many examples of people's names being changed, especially when life changing events occur. This intense transition in my life made me think about my name. What do I want to be called after this experience and how it has affected me? As a non-binary person who uses they/them pronouns, I had already been considering changing my middle name to Noel, but at this point Noel seemed fitting as a first name, as it signifies a new birth.

That's what my chosen family is helping this be for me: a rebirth. I also wanted to think about my last name. I no longer wanted my given last name, but I wanted a name that reminded me that I, a queer human being, belong in this world. I belong with others. With that in mind, I reached out to my friends, who have indeed stayed by my side throughout every part of this leaving and healing process, and I asked, "Can I use part of your last name? I would like to share a last name with both of you." They agreed immediately, and taking parts of their name to form a name of my own reminds me we are family. Sam and Jarrett have saved my life in more ways than one. We may not share our blood. We did not share the same childhood. But we share our queerness and a desire to belong and be a part of a safe, loving community. Because of them, Noel is able to be and see what their future holds.

Luis had doubts about coming out, but he yearned for the authentic life that Christian modeled.

Luis

Storyteller

(he/him)
@itsluisv

Christian

Queer Hand of God

(he/him)

Luis wanted to come out, but feared the backlash. Then he remembered a friend who displayed the courage to live honestly, and followed in his footsteps.

I met Christian through a friend of a friend when we were both closeted. Eventually, Christian came out. I saw how that affected him as a queer Christian person of color. Whenever I thought about coming out, I thought of Christian because of how openly he spoke about his queerness--something I never felt I could do. I asked myself how he could be so comfortable with this part of himself. As time passed, it became harder for me to keep secrets. I wanted to own my story of coming out of the closet. Doubt crept in, telling me I would be cast out if I told anyone. When I didn't know who else to turn to, I remembered Christian. He had come out; how did he cope with the aftermath? He agreed to meet with me, took time to listen, and offered me valuable advice. He inspired me to start living from a place of honesty. Christian helped give me the courage I needed to be true to myself, regardless of what others think. Christian exemplifies Christ's love for me, because God rejoices in the truth.

Brit experiences a Good Samaritan moment that changes her life.

Brit

Storyteller

(she/her)
@britcooperrobinson

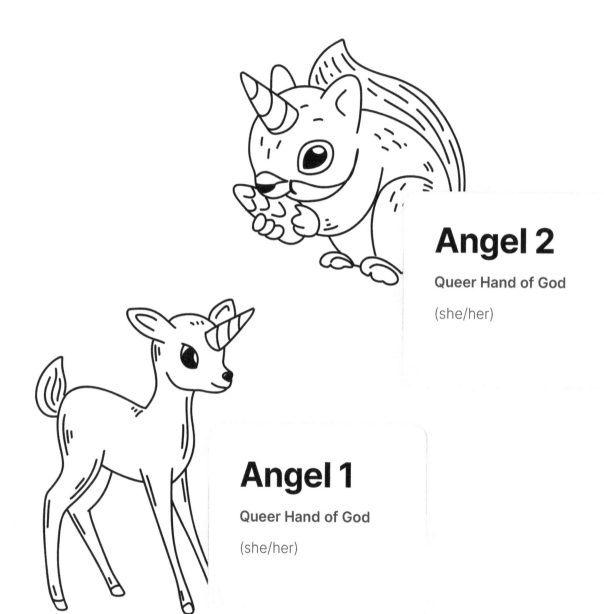

Angel 2

Queer Hand of God

(she/her)

Angel 1

Queer Hand of God

(she/her)

When Brit collapses on a subway platform, she is surprised by who stops to offer her aid. This couple's kindness convicts her and turns her into a true ally.

I was young, new to the city, and didn't yet realize I was spending most of my energy trying to ignore my trauma. One winter morning during my commute, I began to overheat on the packed subway train. There was nowhere to lean and I yanked at my scarf as it started to choke me. I tried to deepen my breathing, like my therapist had instructed, but the sudden awareness of my body just made things worse. The adrenaline was building and I felt trapped. At the next available stop, I frantically shoved my way through the mob of commuters only to collapse on the platform.

As I regained consciousness, I squeezed my eyes tighter while the train platform spun. I was aware of the cold pavement under my face and the rush of people around me. I felt exposed and worried someone might try to take advantage of that. I resisted the urge to vomit and took a deep breath in an attempt to steady myself.

I wanted to lift my head but the dizziness increased with the effort. Minutes dragged out. As someone stepped over me, my panic spiked. Was no one going to help me? How could I be completely surrounded by people and yet, totally alone? As hot tears started gathering behind my eyelids, I heard two voices cut through the buzz of commuters and trains. "I've got her," one said, "I'm calling for help" the other echoed. Then I felt a warm hand slip between my face and the freezing pavement. Her face was kind, surrounded by a flash of spiky blonde hair and maybe half a dozen piercings. She held my head with care and her eyes creased with concern. "It's alright," she said, "my wife is finding help and I'm here. We won't leave until you're okay." During the moments that followed, this lesbian couple created a bubble of calm around me while the rush of the morning commute continued. I was still surrounded by strangers, but I was no longer alone.

In the years since, I've often thought about my gay guardian angels. At the time, I recognized they defied everything my conservative upbringing taught about who loves, who helps, and who knows the Divine. It wasn't lost on me that these two people had, at one point or many, been rejected, hurt, and ignored by society. And yet, here they were, helping a stranger. You're not alone in seeing the parallels between this story and Jesus' parable of the good Samaritan.

I was never taught to identify with the original criminals who beat and robbed the victim, but, the truth is, I grew up benefiting from the communities and cultures that shunned these two women. I had tried to be a neutral party. I didn't want to actively cause harm, but I always stayed out of the way. At best, I had been the person who stepped over them. This couple didn't know that about me, but I wouldn't have blamed them for assuming it. Instead they quietly modeled how to uphold a person's humanity - no questions asked. It would take time before I could fully articulate all this experience taught me but I knew there was no other way forward. It wasn't enough to "not cause harm." I needed to be an active part of repairing it.

I hate that I don't know their names. As the EMT's started checking me, both women stood to leave. I'm sure by then they were late for work. I was dazed, drained, and only mumbled a shaky "thank you." I wish I could give them proper credit in the telling of this story. But if you ever see me, or read my words, or hear what I teach my children, you can know that these two passing strangers left a lasting mark.

Nadia's journey to acceptance of self and others is aided by Kay's gentle but tough love.

Nadia

Storyteller

(she/her)
@nbuserkrus

Kay

Queer Hand of God

(they/them)

Kay is patient with Nadia's questioning, but their self-respect and boundaries are what ultimately make the biggest difference for Nadia's change of heart.

The summer after I graduated from college, I moved across the country to start a year as an AmeriCorps volunteer. I was living in a new town, thousands of miles away from the family and friends I had spent my entire life with. Nervous but excited, I daydreamed about becoming best friends with my new housemates and going on adventures and finding a new church to be a part of. My faith had been my solid rock for all of my teen and adult life, and while it brought me a lot of comfort, unfortunately it was also intertwined with homophobia, transphobia, and a fatalistic trust in "God's will" that translated into apathy about most social justice topics. All of this changed, though, when I met Kay.

Kay was my roommate and the first self-identified queer person I had ever met. We clicked instantly, due to our goofy personalities and love of deep conversation. Within a few weeks, I was thrown into a crisis of faith and identity as I realized that the Catholic teachings I had grown up with told me that Kay was sinful and wrong in embracing their queer identity. I had several conversations with them in which I shared my faith and asked them (in retrospect, very invasive and insensitive questions) about whether they'd ever tried to pray about their sexuality and gender identity and whether they were trying to change. Kay was patient with these questions at first, but as time went on and these conversations began to weigh on their sense of peace and belonging in our home, they asked for space and boundaries in our friendship. They encouraged me to find books to read that presented an affirming perspective on queerness and urged me to talk to another housemate of ours who had also grown up Catholic but had chosen a more affirming spirituality since then.

This space-taking experience was incredibly painful for me, mostly because I had (without admitting it) fallen in love with Kay. I spent the rest of the year reading—unlearning and unpacking the beliefs I had grown up with and learning new ones. I also spent that time coming to terms with the fact that I was going through heartbreak and acknowledging for the first time that I was queer too—a reality I had been suppressing since middle school because I thought that it was sinful for me, as a woman, to love women, and non-binary and trans people.

At first, when I would talk about my connection with Kay, it was a story of sadness, anger, and pain. But as time went on, and I started to come out about my own queer identity, shifted my spiritual beliefs, and began to be an advocate for LGBTQ+ inclusion and affirmation in the church. I also started to date a woman for the first time. As a result, I began to realize how monumental Kay's impact was on my life. They did their best to be gentle and patient with me even when I questioned their identity and hurt them with my ignorance.

Three years after that experience, Kay and I reconnected briefly and reconciled, prompted by Kay reaching out to congratulate me on coming out. This experience broke me open in a painful but ultimately good and life-changing way. These days I am convinced that the key to helping others to become affirming of the LGBTQ+ community is to introduce them to queer people and let them fall in love—even simply as friends—with them, with us. Love wins, not only in our queer relationships but in eradicating the prejudice and fear that keep people stuck in homophobia, transphobia, and exclusion.

Byron's friendship with Father Micah leads him on a similar journey.

Byron

Storyteller

(he/him
@walker_lordbyron

Father Micah

Queer Hand of God

(he/him)
@apptowonder37

Byron was searching for a spiritual home, and Father Micah led the way.

A Sunday evening in August, Father Micah led me through one of the most simple and common Eastern Orthodox prayers during vespers service: "Glory to the Father, and to the Son, and to the Holy Spirit. Both now and ever and unto the ages of ages. Amen." Then he told me to do the sign of the cross. I did. He chuckled. "No, the other way."

These little details matter when you've fought for them as hard as Micah has. Few people know and love their traditions and their faith as deeply as those of us who have wrestled for them, even as Jacob wrestled with God to bless him. The story of being kicked out of a church for being bisexual is sadly a common one, and not everyone who is forced out of a denomination comes back. Even fewer still dig deep with the tenacity of the women disciples who refused to leave Jesus at the cross. Micah pursued the heart of Jesus all the way to the deep and mysterious bosom of Eastern Orthodoxy.

The rich and embodied traditions of Orthodoxy echoed through my memories and came back to me as Micah led me through the prayers. I had grown up in Bethlehem near Jerusalem and some of the oldest and most holy churches in Christianity, many of them Orthodox. These were tied intimately with my earliest religious memories, though years later it was in the shadow of my own expulsion from a Presbyterian church that I first met Micah.

I made his acquaintance at a queer Christian conference in his home state of Colorado, but I got the pleasure of truly getting to know him when he moved to my hometown of Seattle a year later to attend seminary. We got to know each other very well. Few weeks would go by where we weren't meeting up discussing deep theological topics. Frankly, it was impossible for us to be around each other for more than five minutes before we started talking about some delightful topic concerning God. I had so much to learn, and Micah was a patient teacher. No question was ever too strange, and he had some mind-bending and scandalous things for me to learn.

Even so, the journey was not over for him. Little surprise, but the Greek Orthodox church is not the most welcoming tradition to

LGBTQ+ people. Though excommunication doesn't quite mean the same thing in Orthodoxy as it does in Catholic circles, it still stings. Yet, it seems no earthly authority could deter Micah from his God-given call into the clergy.

As we talked, we grew, shared, and discerned our own individual vocations and callings. He quickly became one of my closest friends and has been one of the most significant queer influences on my life. Micah has been the hand of God in my life, serving me and guiding me in my pursuits and thought.

Micah, now properly called Father Micah Lazarus, eventually became a priest in the Universalist Orthodox Church (UOC). The UOC, an open and affirming (and entirely queer led) jurisdiction of the Eastern Orthodox faith, has recently become my ecclesial home, following a faith journey in which I have searched across continents and through centuries of religious traditions and practices. Micah and I have walked this journey together. Every time I had a question, he would explain the orthodox view, and I would consistently resonate with it. At other times, I would be expounding my own theology, and he would remark at how orthodox it sounded. We've shared the experience of rejection from protestant churches, as well as the personal travails of grandparents who just don't seem to get it.

Orthodoxy is in his blood, likely from all the communion he receives and now offers as a minister of word and sacrament. Fr. Micah has changed my life; conveying the body of Christ to me as the very hand of God, and doing it all as his powerfully queer, practical, and curious self. And as Micah always says, we will continue in the hope of Jesus, "the Lord willing and the creek don't rise."

"I had so much to learn, and Micah was a patient teacher. No question was ever too strange, and he had some mind-bending and scandalous things for me to learn."

-Byron

Friendships with those who are different from you have a lot to teach us.

Mason

Storyteller

(he/him)
@masonmenenga

Mark

Queer Hand of God

(he/him)

Joel

Queer Hand of God

(he/him)
@jcarlovsky

Mason's relationship with married couple
Mark and Joel has taught him to be brave
in life and love.

I met Mark and Joel almost 5 years ago, and I haven't been the
same since. Because I grew up in a conservative religious home,
I didn't know anyone who was out, much less married to a
partner of the same gender. I believe Mark and Joel were the
first gay married couple with whom I became friends. One of the
first times we hung out was on a men's retreat with our church.
The word "retreat" is doing a lot of work here, because it was
less of a retreat and more of a bachelor party—culminating in a
brewery tour in a party bus with a stripper pole. Needless to say,
Mark, Joel, and I have spent countless nights slightly inebriated,
dancing to Britney Spears and Weezer. Outside of these wild and
fun evenings together, almost every time I hang out with Mark
and Joel we first hug, say our greetings, and then basically
immediately begin to talk about topics like homophobia, sex, and
faith. These conversations

with Mark and Joel have not only solidified a lifelong friendship, but they have formed who I have become. There are three things in particular from my friendship with Mark and Joel that have made a lasting impact on my life.

Mark and Joel have taught me how to have brave conversations. When I first started having deep conversations with them, I remember being nervous about asking the wrong thing. Whether it is about gay sex, their experiences of homophobia, or even how they've wrestled with their faith and being gay, I have learned to be brave in difficult conversations, especially with friends who are different from me. It is better to ask the wrong thing than not to have open and honest conversations with the people to whom you're closest. In doing so, you will be able to grow more deeply with them.

Mark and Joel have also taught me how to radically rethink my relationships in general. Growing up in a conservative religious home meant that all of my relationships were black and white. I could have only platonic friendships with men and only romantic relationships with women. My platonic friendships had to look a certain way and my romantic relationships had to look a certain way. But by being friends with Mark and Joel I have learned that our relationships aren't so black and white. Mark, Joel, and I talk about sex quite often

Even more, we love to gas each other up when one of us is looking cute or if one of us posts a tasteful selfie. This kind of relationship is much more grey than the kind of black and white relationships I was taught to have growing up. My relationship with Mark and Joel has helped me queer my relationships with everyone. Queerness is not only about the kinds of people one does and doesn't have sex with. It also means radically reimagining all kinds of relationships, including platonic ones. Whether you're queer or not, queerness can teach us so much about all of our relationships.

Lastly, Mark and Joel have taught me to love unapologetically. Within the first few months of meeting Mark and Joel, my conservative parents met them, and I was scared to show the love I had for my two gay married friends in front of my family. But Mark and Joel love me regardless of who I am and I realized in that moment that I should also be unapologetic of my love for them, even if I was going to be judged by family for it. It can be hard to love unapologetically, but we owe it to our loved ones, especially those who are marginalized, to love them even if it means we may be rejected by others. You are deserving of love, as is everyone else, so simply love unapologetically.

Alice finds a role model of integrity and confidence in Stuart.

Alice

Storyteller

(she/her)
@talesofaubergine

Stuart

Queer Hand of God

(he/him)
@stuart.ridley

While she struggled with her own identity and faith, Alice was encouraged by seeing Stuart live his truth.

After the breakdown of my marriage and an unhealthy relationship, I felt very unwelcome in my home church. Add to that my blooming recognition of my bisexuality and the war that came with trying to reconcile my faith, my identity, and what I had been taught (erroneously) about how they related to each other, and I was having a hard time being true to myself and to God.

Stuart was just this pillar of how it was possible to be a believer and live his own truth. We started Sydney's first (and Australia's second) LGBT+ ice hockey club together with a growing crew. I was able to settle more comfortably within my own skin after seeing how it was possible to align your faith and identity without compromising either.

Just knowing that Stuart is a believer who is his truest self has been such an encouragement to me. Faith and identity are not separate things, but both celebrate the other. God celebrates me for all that he made me, and I praise God for all that he has done.

Qiu unexpectedly finds a queer friend at a Christian college.

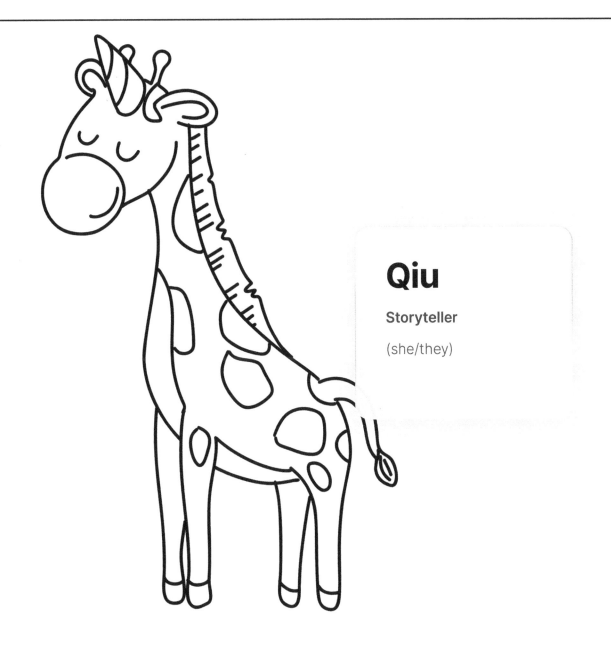

Qiu

Storyteller

(she/they)

Erica

Queer Hand of God

(they/them)
@e_bashyy

Qiu thought she would have to survive college as a queer woman alone, but Erica proved to be an invaluable support.

In the fall of 2019, I was preparing to go a Christian college. I struggled with the idea of being gay and studying there. I knew I was a pansexual Asian woman, and I wasn't sure how I would survive this Christian college experience. My family, however, offered to fund my college education if I attended a Christian college and I couldn't pass on the offer. During my freshman year, I attended a camping trip, and they mentioned one of the leaders, Erica, was queer. I was suprised about this, thinking I would never meet any queer people at the school. I reached out to Erica, a junior, via Facebook Messenger and asked about support. I explained my situation, and they responded to me by inviting me to talk in person and hold space to have casual and theological conversations. Both us were navigating how to be queer at the college, how to combat internalized queerphobia, and these talks brought me great peace. Because of Erica, I was able to dispel false narratives that kept me believing I was not loved by God. Today my faith in God is my own, what others think about my faith does not determine my relationship with God. People don't define my relationship with God. This is between me and God.

Difficult life transitions had AJ doubting and resisting God, but John helped her see clearly.

AJ

Storyteller

(she/her)
@ajtheswift

John

Queer Hand of God

(He/him)

AJ felt disillusioned and isolated from God, John showed her a faith that helped her see God with new eyes.

I'd been in church my whole life, and I came out after the Pulse mass shooting. I was working as a hairdresser in my very conservative hometown and felt bombarded with messages of gay hate from the public. I started mocking Christians as a way to prevent myself from getting hurt. To make matters worse, my health was declining. I was dehydrated and depressed; I would wake up in the middle of the night and had trouble sleeping, and my energy was low. I was taught that God would heal me if he wanted, but nothing was happening. I didn't feel respected at my work and my interest dwindled. I envisioned myself working in a new industry.

I joined believr early on and met John. I felt he was pretentious. He was very positive about the Bible, and I resisted this in return, thinking that the Bible was the very channel used to hurt others.

But John showed me such kindness and softness. He made an analogy about the Bible. He said it was like braille, and it helps us feel our way to God. As time passed, I began to align myself to Christ. Different doors began to open. My health had returned, and my body had more energy and more peace. I had gotten a new job, and I felt that God placed me in the perfect team. Things just felt easier. It felt as if something was watching over me and caring for me. Today I feel God as a blind person would read, running their fingers through a braille message.

"He made an analogy about the Bible. He said it was like braille, and it helps us feel our way to God."

-AJ

After struggling to fit into church spaces, Andrew finds a welcoming pastor.

Andrew

Storyteller

(he/him)

Pastor Katie

Queer Hand of God

(she/her)
@thewellqueenanne

Andrew wasn't sure he would ever find a Christian space that felt like home, but then he met Pastor Katie, who showed him evangelical Christianity wasn't the only option.

I make my way towards El Diablo Coffee in Seattle, Washington, feeling shaky and anxious. I had asked a friend if he knew of a minister who had been involved in progressive Christianity for a while. I needed a mentor with real experience in liberative religion because I wanted to figure out a way back into church community life.

There are butterflies in my stomach as I question myself about being vulnerable in this way. Is this person going to judge me? Am I cool or hip enough to be up to the standards of the kind of church that affirms LGBTQ people and marches in the streets with Black Lives Matter?

Seattle has a toxic history when it comes to church life. One example is the patriarchal, queerphobic, controlling, vegan-hating Mark Driscoll and his church, Mars Hill. I was fortunate enough to sniff out the toxicity there when I went once in the late 90's.

No thank you. I wanted to be a part of a religious life that was open to everybody and working for justice in my beloved hometown. Unfortunately, I didn't know where to seek out such a place.

I grew up in Christian communes in Seattle, Honolulu, Los Angeles, and then Mazatlan, Mexico in the 80's and 90's. These were (somewhat) inclusive communities that emphasized practical love and devoted spiritual life. It was later, in my high school years, that I began to encounter a more negative, judgmental, and hypocritical type of Christianity at youth group. I was bombarded with contemporary Christian pop artists like DC Talk and Carman telling me what to do with my mind and my body. I couldn't stand these groups, mostly because their music was so bad, but it was also this "purity culture" that rubbed me the wrong way.

Still, despite my dislike of so many of these environments, the "Spirit" got into me. The words of Jesus, the apostles, and the prophets resonated. I wanted to have a life of meaning, love people, create community, work for justice in the world. I projected all of this into the possibility of the Church. Through the next ten years of life, through internships and ordained ministry, I learned that the church, as I then knew it, was not for me.

I walk into El Diablo Coffee, and I look for "Pastor Katie." What I know about Katie is this: she is married to a woman, is from the South, and has been out and in ministry with the United Methodist Church since the 90's. This is an individual with legit "queer, progressive Christian" cred. This is the kind of person I want approval from so badly.

My own Christian adventure had ended in traumatic loss. Through a series of events starting with the American war response to 9/11, I realized that I was, or was becoming, a leftist. Becoming a leftist was directly connected to my understanding of Jesus, the apostles, and the prophets. It was directly related to how my missionary mother taught me that the Spirit was working through MLK and the Civil Rights Movement and through resisters of the Nazis in WW2. This was the same Spirit that worked through abolitionists and suffragettes, in prison reformers and proponents of humane labor laws.

What about injustice in our time? Why did evangelical leaders say that queer people couldn't be Christians? Some would say you could be gay or lesbian as long as you were celibate, but that is not an actual embrace of queer people. I knew this and realized that there was an end date for me in evangelical Christianity. I never identified with that label anyway. But what could I do then? Where could I go? At that time, that meant leaving church altogether. And that is what I did. I left the ministry for the next ten years while feeling like an absolute failure. I picked up the pieces and tried to rebuild some kind of life outside of the church.

Pastor Katie arrives at the coffee shop. She has a very nice, gracious smile. She asks me about my life and story. She laughs, in a nice way, when I discuss some of the evangelical garbage that I had gotten rid of over the years. The reason that she laughs is not because of mockery, but because of her own ignorance of evangelical culture. Pastor Katie never really experienced any of that. She grew up in this other type of Christianity that I had only read about. This was the liberal, progressive branch of American religion, where women were leaders, queer people were affirmed, racial justice was prioritized, and pretty much nobody listened to DC Talk or Carman.

Everybody else I knew who was in evangelical circles seemed to go in a few basic directions: lean into conservative Christianity; leave the church and forget about it altogether; or live with bitterness and a visceral hatred of Christianity. None of those were ever options for me. The impact of the words and Spirit of Jesus and all those Bible characters were imprinted onto my bones and soul. To deny that would be to deny my own self.

And here was Pastor Katie. Welcoming me.

Now I could be with Pastor Katie, a woman married to a woman and pastoring a local church, and I could embrace my ambiguous sense of gender and sexuality. I can lean into the concept that there are an infinite number of genders. That makes sense to me, even if it doesn't make sense to a whole lot of other people in this country and in the church.

With Pastor Katie, I didn't have to have all the answers. I could just *be*, and talk with her about horror movies, politics, dreams, theology, personal life. Pastor Katie was open to getting to know me. I was open to getting to know her.

It took me over a year of meeting with Katie until I felt comfortable going to church. Six months later I became an official member. I feel very much like I can live without having all the answers about myself. I can love the neighbor, make art, be on fire for justice.

Thank you Pastor Katie!

Lorae is surprised by a work acquaintance who becomes an ambassador of God's grace.

Lorae

Storyteller

(she/her)
@loraevb

Cory

Queer Hand of God

(he/him)

Cory enters Lorae's office and her life and becomes a close friend.

I am sitting in the windowless office of my new job in the summer of 2018, with a space heater running because it is freezing here. It feels like a meat locker. I am aimlessly moving my mouse around to make sure no one gives me any busy work, and in walks a 6'2" ball of sunshine. He has on rainbow Tevas, a patterned short-sleeve shirt with a collar, and khaki shorts that stop mid-thigh. He is carrying a shoulder bag and breezes by three offices in approximately five steps. He comes by the office a few times a week for the rest of the summer, and before I know it, I am sitting across from him, interviewing him to be my supervisor. November 7th, 2018 was the beginning of a supervisory relationship that would turn to friendship and mentorship and change the trajectory of my life—I thank God for Cory.

There is no one moment or one encounter that changed me, but it is everything about who he is that tells me that nothing is by happenstance, and that God is intentional. Psalm 68:6 reminds me that God places the lonely in families, [They] set the prisoners free and give them joy, but the rebellious live in a sun-scorched land. Through his radical love and candor, Cory showed me a world full of color that I could bravely traverse in order to stand in my full truth as a queer Black woman. He modeled the way for me to see how one can exist in difficult familial relationships. He showed me what it means to center my queerness and other marginalized social identities in my career, and he never judged me or rushed me in my process. Most of all, he advocated for me fiercely and believed in me a thousand times more than I ever believed in myself.

He told me I was a brilliant writer. He spoke life into me about my future work and scholarship, and he kicked down every door in front of me to ensure I had the best chance at succeeding in my career and life. I remember when I showed him pictures of the woman I'd eventually marry. He told me she was stunning and celebrated with me. He never questioned me when I was living in tension and struggle, and he was always a safe place for me to express my deepest fears. My relationship with Cory started off as a supervisory relationship, but now I cannot imagine my life without him. He is a dear friend sent by the Most High to bring more love into my life.

I never wanted to move two hours away from my family of origin to start a new job. I actually cried for the three weeks prior to my move and then cried some more when my supervisor that hired me left three months into my time here. But God was orchestrating something I could not fathom in my wildest dreams. They would bring someone to me who would help me untangle the harmful and violent messaging I'd received through my upbringing in church, while still maintaining a deep appreciation for the spiritual. Someone who would be a co-conspirator with me in all things social justice, and also be a mentor and teacher and friend. They sent someone who saw me through a difficult period in my life, and was ready to cheer me on and celebrate me when the morning came. It sounds a lot like Jesus, right? That's who Cory is. A person who does not necessarily identify as Christian, but lives with a Christ consciousness stronger than anyone else I know.

I know that the Most High was in this interaction because this relationship has brought healing, clarity, growth, peace, freedom, and abundance, and good trees bear good fruit.

Cory is a good man, and I feel blessed and honored that God would choose me to experience friendship with him. I remember praying for deep friendships on a bus to a Christian college student conference in 2015, and I never thought that the prayer would still be answered for years to come, but Cory is evidence that it is.

"...and I never thought that the prayer would still be answered for years to come, but Cory is evidence that it is."

-Lorae

Emma-Claire explores the expansiveness of queer friendship on the road.

Emma-Claire

Storyteller

(she/her)
@e.c.l.a.i.r.e.

Sasha

Queer Hand of God

(she/her)

While on a roadtrip with Sasha, Emma-Claire experiences the life-giving love of queer friendship.

On our way to the world's largest can of tomato soup, billboard Jesus glared down at us from his wooden perch beside a highway running through Ohio. We'd been on the road through rural America for some time now and had experienced our fair share of Christian fear marketing (my favorite being the *Concerned? Jesus is the way!* billboard that had me wondering if Jesus would do my taxes, clean my kitchen, and take care of every other concern in my life) but this one promised more. It promised adventure.

And that adventure was BibleWalk: Ohio's only Biblical wax museum.

With only three miles until the exit, we couldn't resist. We rerouted Google Maps and pulled into a multi-building compound with a nearly empty parking lot, and from the moment we stepped out of the car it seemed even the trees were staring at us, noticing how much we didn't belong. This was the appeal, the adrenaline, the irresistible urge to analyze and laugh at something designed to harm us. Straight people have B-movie horror films; we have heartland Christianity.

I hadn't known Sasha very long, but she had quickly become one of my favorite friends. Queer people are like this, U-hauling friendship and going on cross-country road trips with someone you met online. As we approached the front desk, we could see in the receptionist's bespeckled eyes that this might just be the first time two visibly queer people had ever walked through her doors. Here was Sasha, with her men's cuffed jeans, a beanie and oversized jacket; here was me, with my pink hair and flannel; and here was the receptionist, with her pastel blouse and elegant broach, ushering us into a room where we would finally find out *how to get into heaven.*

We looked at each other while standing in front of wax Jesus, hanging from his wax cross, with no nipples for some reason, built to strike our hearts with the fear of a hell we'd been taunted with our whole lives. We laughed at post-resurrection wax Jesus, riding on his wax horse, wearing his gold crown and pageant sash, just one bold lip away from full drag.

My whole life I heard the church condemn the sin of "practicing homosexuals," forbidding any romance beyond the boundaries of heterosexuality. But here in the dim lighting of the BibleWalk, our presence felt subversive for reasons having nothing to do with romance or sex. The church has been so busy preaching fire and brimstone about who we love that they have entirely missed the true essence of the queer experience: *how* we love.

Sasha showed me that being queer is far too expansive to be defined by who you are or are not sleeping with, a favorite definition of bigoted opponents and misguided allies alike. The existential humor she moved through life with made me feel seen in ways I couldn't articulate, but that was okay because who needs words when you're hiking through the canyons of Utah, when you're watching the moon sink below the desert horizon. She gave me the courage to wonder if all the other parts of my life that I'd always wondered about, the parts that made me feel different from my peers, the parts that never quite fit in with the society around me—*could those parts be queer too? Even if they had nothing to do with attraction?*

We listened to the soundtrack of every episode of Glee as we drove through the empty plains of Kansas. We took a wrong turn in sunny Colorado and ended up in a mountain blizzard. We added a piece of twine to the world's largest ball of it, and all of this was queer somehow.

Sasha's confidence in who she was emanated through every time zone and called me into deeper understanding of self, of neighbor, and of the divine. We hear stories all the time of queer awakenings being sparked by cartoon characters and pixie-cut actresses, moments of sexual attraction that are important and good but on their own don't paint a full picture of all that queerness can be. No one had prepared me for this moment, this awakening that comes from queer friendship, this shattering of every way the world had ever worked.

After our tour through the life and death of wax Jesus, we walked past a mural depicting some people walking peacefully to heaven next to some people tossing themselves into hell. We know this mural was meant to scare us, and we joked about being magically made straight by the power of vibrant acrylic on canvas, but looking back on it I can't help but wonder how this transcendent definition of being queer breaks down the old eschatologies.

If being queer is just about who you love, then sure, every same-sex couple gets a one-way ticket downstairs. But if being queer is about *how* you love, and how you live, then how can we divide people into the supposedly easy binaries of saved and damned?

Does loving Sasha with a love stronger than heteronormative friendship condemn my eternal soul, even if we never so much as hold hands? How do you categorize the kind of intimacy that can only be lived out through packing a small car with way too many suitcases each morning in a cheap motel parking lot, while studying for finals, while drinking 40 capri suns, while dreaming out loud of our plans to spend the summer working with queer youth and young adults?

The stories we have of queer romantic love are beautiful and important. I could write about the women I have known and loved in this way. But far less celebrated are these love stories of friendships, these odes to the ones who taught us how to be queer just by teaching us how to be our true selves. Sasha was queer in the way she dressed, in the way she encouraged my new habit of buying trucker hats at each souvenir shop, in the way she told me her life story as east coast trees blurred into west coast canyons.

I'm currently in seminary studying youth ministry, outdoor education, and queer theology. I am relentless in my refusal to be kicked out of a place that has no right not to welcome me on the basis of who and how I love. We humans have an incredible capacity for love, and if our love cannot be put in a box than neither can God's.

I met the divine out on the road. How small it must feel to worship a God made of wax, immovable, stoic, caged behind a velvet rope. I follow the God who showed up that week in the face of my friend. She was made in God's image—how could I not love her? How could you call this cross-country friendship anything less than love?

"She showed me that being queer is far too expansive to be defined by who you are or are not sleeping with..."

-Emma-Claire

T's preaching shows Chavonn a new way to be Christian.

Chavonn

Storyteller

(she/they)
@chavonnwshen

T

Queer Hand of God

(he/him)

Chavonn found home and inspiration in T's radical queer church and life.

"Jesus must've been a profound disappointment to those around him," said the preacher at this church that I had just discovered.

"He had no military experience, wasn't rich, or even from an influential family. But he was telling people to love their enemies and bless those who curse you? What's up with that?"

I was hooked. This was the first time I'd ever heard Jesus expressed as anything other than the Ultimate Being that everyone must've loved, except for the Romans or others who had twisted views of religion. But that one sermon put Jesus in a very relatable, very human, context. That one sermon allowed me to bring the doubts that I had as a queer, Black, disabled femme about this whole Jesus thing and put them squarely in the context of other very relatable, very human, people who had been disappointed in what Jesus was not. But even more, the sermon left me with a sense of wonder. The sermon's major takeaway was that even if I had been disappointed by what Christianity was, that didn't mean that I couldn't look for the thread of liberation and love for marginalized people woven within the story and see it borne out in my own life.

I absolutely loved that sermon. So I went to that church the next week. And the week after. And the week after. It took over a month for me to work up the nerve to tell the pastor that I liked his sermons and that I had never heard Christians called to activism in the ways he described. But what I didn't say is that his sermons saved my faith, which I was on the verge of losing due to my church of origin's reaction to my sexuality. I also didn't tell him I thought he was super cool and that I wanted to be his friend. After subsequent conversations, I learned this preacher, T, was a gay Chinese American who founded his church based on ecological racial justice and the belief that the queer people and BIPOC are the true revolutionaries. He made his church into a space where the most marginalized didn't just have a barely-there seat at the table, but a space that celebrates them and gives them room to thrive in ways that I didn't even know could exist.

T is constantly showing me through his actions how to move as a child of God and how to look for the light of God in every person, no matter how hard it may be. His unapologetic queerness has explicitly encouraged me to live into my own. He has changed my life theologically, interpersonally, and creatively, in ways that make me want to be my best queer Christian self for myself and for others.

In a time of transition, Nathaniel meets Rev. John McLeon, whose journey and character made him a model of Christ.

Elliot

Queer Hand of God

(he/him)
@elliotsgreen

Nathanial

Queer Hand of God

(she/her)

Rev. John

Queer Hand of God

(she/her)

Rev. John McLeon's experience as a gay minister throughout the decades made him a kind and caring person, who Nathaniel came to love, respect, and look up to.

In the early spring of 2018, I was nearing the end of my senior year at Liberty University. Standing between my exasperated self and liberation from the institution was an outstanding internship requirement, one I had gone to great lengths to get. Two previous opportunities had already fallen through, one as the consequence for coming out and the other for financial limitations, so I was anxiously anticipating an internship I hoped would come through, one that required me to move to Nashville, Tennessee, to spend a summer serving at GracePointe Church in their Creative Arts department.

Liberty required my internship to consume 400 hours over 10-12 weeks, and given GracePointe's limited gathering schedule for the summer, I anticipated difficulty finding 40 hours per week of work to do. While visiting my family in Michigan that spring,

I received a call from an enthusiastic man who introduced himself as Rev. John McLean. He was the minister for Unity of Nashville, another religious organization, and he was interested in my availability to assist him and his staff with some office and property work while I lived there. I was elated, but more than anything, I was relieved. Unity could supplement my work with GracePointe, and they also possessed space in their office building that they would let me live in for the summer without charge.

I moved to Nashville on May 26th, 2018, making my home in the upstairs bedroom of the church office. The campus was beautiful, and I was instantly captivated by the attention to natural spaces evident on the property. From the gardens around the entryway to the prayer labyrinth in the rear, the intentionality of Unity's caretakers was clear. I had no idea what I would be stepping into, but my hands and heart were open. The unknown felt promising to me.

Little did I know the gift this opportunity would be.

I first met Rev. John that following Monday in his office, finding myself instantly charmed by his earnest enthusiasm. I've often struggled to describe Rev. John to those who don't know him, in large part due to how rare of a person he is. Sometimes I describe him as a seminary-trained Nathan Lane. A man in his mid-60s with white hair and broad-rimmed glasses, Rev. John will emphatically insist on how much he loves getting "old." He regularly wears bowties with his suits, eschewing bland palettes for vibrancy and exuberance. I've lost count of the number of times I heard him singing music from artists and eras unknown to me, but he lives his life in song and dance and color.

Rev. John once shared that he grew up in the 1960s believing he would die in Vietnam as a young gay kid. In the 1970s, he lived his dream in Washington, D.C., working for a United States Senator by the name of Ted Kennedy. A believer in public service, he's spent his life working in the interest of, as he puts it, saving the world. He didn't attend seminary until after his partner died, and it was through this journey that he became a minister in the Unity movement.

The more I learned about him and through him, the more I came to understand just how profoundly he was shaped by grief. Facing unimaginable loss in a time of outright hostility to his identity and experiences, Rev. John believed wholeheartedly in a faith that was just and liberating, and he was committed to cultivating radical belonging.

Rev. John brings his true and authentic self to bear in every situation, and every person who shares space with him is better for it.

Working Sunday services in the tech booth was where I witnessed Rev. John's applied philosophy of ministry and learned, for myself, a new way of approaching church. Unity's teachings are different from my tradition's, but I was never anything other than grateful to have been invited into the community. I learned a great deal from their methods, and found myself looking forward to Sunday mornings. Services were preceded by moments of contemplative silence and meditation, and silence itself was a regular part of the liturgical order. While I was technically on the clock, I felt that I benefited in my mental and emotional health, feeling grounded by every service.

One of the details that has stuck with me from those summer Sundays is the manner in which Rev. John introduced himself each week: "I'm Rev. John McLean, and it's the delight of my life to serve as Senior Minister here at Unity of Nashville."

It was neither the exact words nor the context in which he said them that surprised me—it was that he meant every one of them.

Having sat through an incalculable number of megachurch services in my life, I've observed the performative positivity any pastor can put forward on stage. There have been few times, however, where the act of introducing oneself has left me moved to tears. Each week, even in the busy-ness of office work, it was never anything other than clear to me that he loved his job and savored the work of ministry.

His love for his work and his community, and his earnest optimism for the future grounded me in my faith and calling at a time of prevailing uncertainty.

It was later that summer that my then-fiancé, Elliot, moved in with me. For several weeks until we had our own apartment, we called the upstairs bedroom of Unity of Nashville our home. Neither of us had the support of our families, and having just relocated to a new city, there were few friends we could call on on such short notice to join us for the occasion.

When it came time to plan a ceremony, we quickly agreed that Rev. John was the ideal officiant. While we'd only known him a short time, his impact on our lives was significant. He agreed to officiate our ceremony, and in the prayer labyrinth at Unity of Nashville on the afternoon of September 29th, 2018, Rev. John conducted the most beautiful service of marriage I'd ever experienced. He had written most of the material himself, and apart from the beauty of the words, it was knowing him and his journey that gave the occasion a gravity it otherwise wouldn't have had. This gay pastor in the South, having loved and lived and lost more than most, charged us to remember that life is *for us*. He gave us a copy of his order of service, and we keep it among our most treasured documents.

Rev. John stepped aside as the senior minister at Unity of Nashville in September of 2021. Elliot and I had the privilege of attending his "de-installation" service, as he called it, and it was the first time we had seen him since the onset of the pandemic. The experience was a profound reminder to me of the gratitude I have to and for him.

When I think of what it means to love with care and authenticity, I think of Rev. John McLean. When I consider what it means to be present in all things, I remember what it's like to be in the presence of Rev. John. When I reflect on Christ's command to love God and love my neighbor as myself, I look to Rev. John as an example to follow.

I wouldn't be who I am today if not for his generosity.

But in our pain is an alchemical choice: we can choose to transmit or transform our hurt. And Serena lives a life of transformation. Although she had few queer Asian American role models in her own growing-up journey, she is comfortable with her own visibility and works to ensure the visibility of her kin so that today's young queer Asian Americans have role models. She co-leads workshops on queer Asian family dynamics, has generously told her story to the benefit of those who might see her, and facilitates online queer Asian Christian communities with tenderness and deftness.

And whereas she has experienced broken covenants from her family of origin, she has chosen a path of love for her own family—co-raising with her wife two children who are gentle, kind, and affirmed of their parents' wide-open love. At the same time, she leaves the door open for the possibility, without expectation, of a healing relationship with her own parents. It's this fierce devotion to love and non-attachment to expectation that have provided a blueprint for my own healing relationship with my family of origin. And it's Serena's own family that has shown my mother that my own is someday possible, God willing.

Serena lives out countless queer spiritual gifts, and she especially embodies the queer spiritual gift of alchemy. This is a magic that God has gifted us queer beloveds: the power to transform experiences of exclusion and pain into kinship and kin-dom.

Voices of others encourage Rebecca to stay in the Church when she's not sure she can.

Rebecca B.

Storyteller

(she/her)
rebecca.brothers.1920

Talia

Queer Hand of God

(she/her)

As a bisexual Christian, Rebecca has faced conflict in the Church, but has also found encouragement to claim her own rightful space in it.

I first met my friend Talia in January 2019, at a brunch for local LGBTQIA+ folks and their allies. When she asked where I went to school, I said, "Walla Walla University. It's a small religious college in southeastern Washington State."

Talia said, "Oh, I know Walla Walla."

I thought she meant the city, so I said, "I guess technically my alma mater is near Walla Walla, in a little town called College Place."

She looked at me and said, "Oh no, I know Walla Walla University. I grew up Seventh-day Adventist."

I said, "Wait. What? So did I!"

She said, "Yeah, my dad was an Adventist pastor."

I said, "No way! So is mine!"

Several months later, Talia told me that after that first meeting, she went out to her car, called a friend, and said, "I have met a rare bird: the bi daughter of an Adventist pastor."

I came out on Twitter years ago, and started coming out to friends in 2017. I came out on Instagram very obliquely in June 2019, and to my parents the following September. It's an ongoing, never-ending process, like painting the Golden Gate Bridge or keeping a sourdough starter alive.

The more I talked with Talia and learned about the trail she's blazed ahead of me and so many queer Adventist-raised folks, the more boldness I gained. I used to be so quiet and good. I used to keep my questions to myself.

I don't have that problem anymore. The more I learn about the history and struggles of my LGBTQIA+ siblings, the easier it is for me to speak out. As Archbishop Desmond Tutu put it, "If you are neutral in situations of injustice, you have chosen the side of the oppressor.

If an elephant has its foot on the tail of a mouse and you say that you are neutral, the mouse will not appreciate your neutrality."

So here is what I want to tell the elephants: Hello. Hi. I'm an LGBTQIA+ Christian. That's not an oxymoron. We are real. We exist. We share your sanctuaries, your potluck tables, your hymnals. We are equally and ardently beloved children of God.

In the wake of Rachel Held Evans' death in May 2019, a fellow bi Christian named Kimmy wrote on Twitter that Evans' words had encouraged her in her faith: "Sister, it is 1000% okay if you leave, but you are also allowed to stay. They cannot take this from you."

Even in my beloved global Episcopal Church, I have met with opposition to my existence. I have seen willful ignorance and foot-dragging from those who think that LGBTQIA+ issues don't really affect their fellow church members, that we don't really need to think about such matters, that these issues aren't worth "splitting the church" over.

Again: Hello. Hi. I'm here, with many others like me. We are your siblings in Christ, and these are our issues. They are very real to us. They affect where we can be employed, what vendors we can use if we get married, whether we can be foster or adoptive parents, whether we can exist—much less hold hands—in public without fear of violence. These issues can affect the quality of the medical care, counseling care, and spiritual care we receive.

If these issues mean nothing to you—if you can socialize with me and others like me, and learn about the unique problems we face, and still say, "Meh"—then I don't know what to tell you. As one Twitter user put it, "I don't know how to explain to you that you should care about other people."

Some days, it is so tempting to leave Christianity. Some days, it is so tempting to cave in to some Christians' insistence that LGBTQIA+ folks have no place in the Church.

But I have to remember: I am allowed to stay. No one can take this from me —the community I find in church, the friendships I have developed through church, the ministry opportunities church gives me, the myriad ways I continue to strengthen my relationship with God through church.

So today, because of people like Talia, and so many others, I am staying in the Church. I suspect I will stay tomorrow too. I'll keep you posted, though.

*An adaptation of Teresa of Avila's prayer

Christ has no body but yours,

No hands, no feet on earth but yours,

Yours are the eyes with which (they see) compassion on this world,

Yours are the feet with which (they) walk to do good,

Yours are the hands, with which (they) bless all the world.

Yours are the hands, yours are the feet,

Yours are the eyes, you are (their) body.

Christ has no body now but yours,

No hands, no feet on earth but yours,

Yours are the eyes with which (they see) compassion on this world.

Christ has no body now on earth but yours.

- Teresa of Avila

THE END

Our Bible App

Helping LGBTQ+ people find their way to the spiritual wellness they deserve.

Until now, it has been extremely difficult to find devotionals, podcasts, and resources that aren't overtly conservative in nature. Our Bible App is here to provide a platform with the largest compilation of progressive faith-based media content, bringing together writers and readers in one final media hub. We hope you will enjoy our offerings. Come back often to discover weekly featured devotionals, podcasts, and more.

ourbibleapp.com    Download on the **App Store**    GET IT ON **Google Play**

believr.

The home for LGBTQ+ Christians to find connection, belonging, and love.

Everyone has inherent value and is worthy of connection, regardless of who they love or what their faith is. believr helps you uncover your personal values using our research-based evaluation. We then use those values to connect you to others, whether for friendships or dating. Find belonging with others while talking about what matters to you, whether one-on-one or in our group Community Spaces. Celebrate all of who you are on believr.

believr.app

CPSIA information can be obtained
at www.ICGtesting.com
Printed in the USA
LVHW071653270122
709448LV00004B/72